CANNIBAL CASSEROLE

New and Selected Poems

Julia Vinograd

Art by Chris Trian

Zeitgeist Press

Cover photo: Hew Wolff

Cover design: Bruce Isaacson

Art by Chris Trian

ISBN: 0-929730-78-X

Zeitgeist Press
1630 University Avenue #34
Berkeley, CA 94703 U.S.A.

Orders & information at:
www.zeitgeist-press.com

CONTENTS

EYES ON TOOTHPICKS

STEWED SOULS

FULL PAGE DRAWINGS:

EYES ON TOOTHPICKS

SERIAL KILLERS

There's a deck of cards of serial killers now,
imagine telling fortunes with them
or playing poker.
The radio talk-show hosts are horrified.
The victims' families are horrified,
everyone's fascinated.
I wouldn't mind owning a copy myself
though I'd no more dare buy one
than I dared check *Story of O* out of the library
when I was 13 and the librarian
was mother-in-law of the Sphinx.
I don't think it will stop with cards either.
I expect the whole Garfield and Batman pageant—
coffee cups and calendars and bathroom mats.
Imagine getting out of the tub
and drying off with a Jack the Ripper towel
while standing on Charlie Manson's face.
I must confess I like it.
Imagine Jeffrey Dahmer magnets for the icebox.
I'm only surprised it took this long.
Our heroes have failed us.
T.V. evangelists and politicians tell us to send money
and it will be all right.
But there isn't enough money and it won't.
So we go to the jails, the madhouse,
the serial killers who never compromise
their own darkness.
Asked the damned about God.
They know.

FOR A FRIEND ARRESTED AT THE DEMONSTRATION

"I spent the last 14 hours in jail," he announced,
all grinning and rumpled, black unwashed curls.
Heroes get coffee, I got him coffee.
"Tell me about it," I asked.
"Well," he gulped his macchiato with both hands
"we were in the street and I couldn't see anyway
so I thought: I'll do a Ginsberg
so I sat down, crossed my legs and put my hands out
and pretty soon we were all holding hands.
And then the mounted police came
and I was sitting in front of a horse.
You know," he interrupted himself with a small sip of coffee,
"a horse really is hung like a horse.
I thought it was just a way of talking.
They packed us into vans and separated men and women
at the holding station. We all sang God Bless America,
it made the guards wonderfully grumpy
and the girls all sang Itsy Bitsy Spider
they must've been beautiful girls
to make Itsy Bitsy Spider ring like the Liberty Bell.
We talked all night like Socrates or Kerouac or Bugs Bunny,
even in jail no-one could catch us.
But jail food sucks, in the morning I got out
and got myself breakfast and wrote this poem."
His yellow notepaper sent lines spinning like frisbees.
Then the coffeehouse door burst open
and a 19 year old girl, bare feet, bare arms
short black hair, short black dress bounced in out of breath.
"Hey you guys," she insisted, "do either of you have a condom?"
"Yeah," my friend said, a little shook, "do you want 2?"
She gave him a special just-for-you smile.
"Oh yes," she said and ran out.
"Freedom", I sighed and drank my coffee.
"Oh yes," he said and watched the light
dancing where her footprints had been.

IF JERUSALEM WERE FRESH BREAD

They knead her with their fists like dough,
armies, kitchens.
They bake her in the oven of their hatred,
in the oven of their love
and cannot tell the difference.
They take her out and into their arms,
there's no smell like fresh bread
and fill their mouths with her stones
and live forever and die forever
and cannot tell the difference.
There are ovens in her memory
but not for bread.
If Jerusalem were fresh bread
for every little family, for weddings,
for festivals
the first thing they do
still wearing their aprons
with dinner places set
and slim candles lit
is reach for a big knife
to slice her in pieces
and then each other,
and cannot tell the difference.

4

WORLD TRADE CENTER

I am an old woman in a black dress
kneeling in the ruins, clutching my shoulders,
teeth clenched and lips drawn back in a snarl,
rocking back and forth in grief and rage.
I need to tear out my enemy's throat.
The taste of his lifeblood is better than strawberries.
I am kneeling in the ruins of Byzantium.
I am kneeling in the ruins of New York.
I am saying the names of my dead children
over and over, as if they were silver bullets
to shoot at God's smile,
but I want to kill my enemy's children
more than I want my own children back.
My face is twisted and strong.
People in uniforms want me to stand up
and get out of their way. I ignore them.
The sky's a pillar of smoke above me.
There's a pillar of fire raging inside me.
I clench my shaking old hands into fists.
I need to squeeze my enemy's throat
more than I need to hold my lover in the sweet and warm.
His body's in front of me, squashed to a bloody pulp
with fallen metal.
Somebody takes our picture.
I am kneeling in the ruins of Jerusalem.
I am kneeling in the ruins of Ireland.
I am kneeling in the ruins of New York.
I am kneeling in the ruins of Stonehenge
that was a city once.
This was a world once
and I was human once but I've forgotten it.
I walk on bloody feet thru war.
Dying soldiers kneel to me
and I smile.

BESIDE MYSELF—HOW I BECAME THE BUBBLELADY

People's Park made me the Bubblelady.
There was going to be a huge street battle
the next day, everyone was mad, I was mad,
but I was a pacifist and besides
if I threw a rock I'd probably hit my foot.
But I wanted to throw something.
I wasn't a very peaceful pacifist.
So I decided to fill a shopping bag
with bottles of soap bubbles
and stay up all night blowing bubbles in the park
and if they wanted to arrest me, fine.
I'd planned a one night symbolic protest.
So that evening I went to the park
and told the 2 rookie cops left to guard it
what I was going to do,
expecting handcuffs at any moment.
They were young, large and bored,
they pretty much shrugged.
The overhead streetlights were on,
 bubbles look different at night.
After about 20 minutes one of the rookies asked
"Hey, can we try?"
I couldn't believe it, I mean they were cops,
but I handed them each a bottle
and damned if they didn't start a contest.
"Mine's bigger than yours."
"Yeah, but look at mine move,
it's the motion that counts."
I quote. I do not comment.
Then a cop car circling the block screeched to a halt
and an officer about 50, also large.
stalked over to us demanding what the hell.
Maybe he thought I'd dosed his rookies,

this was the 60s, after all.
One of the rookies offered him a bottle of bubbles.
He snorted that he didn't play childish games,
turned on his heel and left
while the other rookie commented,
not lowering his voice all that much:
"he's just scared cause his would be too small to see."
Again, I only quote.
The rest of the night was a blur.
I'd only planned the one night
and thought it would end in jail.
I'm not very brave,
but it was for the park, this park
that's always in trouble, with a bad rap,
and when I show it to people
they don't understand.
The next day I took the bubbles on the street.
If they work on cops they'll work on anyone
and little kids started calling me Bubblelady
and the rest is history.
When I look at the park in winter,
all cold and muddy in the rain,
I see my soap bubbles under the earth
with daffodil bulbs, tulips, snowdrops,
waiting for spring.
And sometimes I see the young faces
of those rookies
still playing their game.

ADVENTURE IN A NIGHTCLUB

In a packed roaring nightclub where the bands never stopped
there was a small dark octopus
hiding in the ladies' toilet
and reaching up one curly puckered tentacle
to grope the girls' bright bare butts
when they sat down.
The girls jumped up and screamed
but by the time anyone came
(it was a very loud nightclub)
the octopus had sunk out of sight.
The girls didn't know what had happened
but couldn't stop babbling, they sounded crazy.
Most of them got 86d for being obviously stoned
and causing trouble.
It could have gone on forever.
But once, when a gaggle of girls
were doing coke in the bathroom there was a raid
and all the drugs got flushed down the toilet
and the octopus swallowed them.
Then he didn't know what happened.
His timing was ruined.
After the next girl he forgot to sink out of sight,
just stayed with half his tentacles
waving helplessly over the toilet
while the bouncer's jaw dropped.
The manager called animal control
but before they took the octopus away
to some environmentally correct place
with no more naked bottoms
the manager took the octopus's picture
and hung it over the toilet.
He liked to think of girls
who wouldn't give him a second look
trembling each time they sat down.

READING

When I first loved reading as a young girl
I refused to believe books *had* authors.
Some grumpy old man or tailored coat lady
invented the lover I took to bed last night
and was leering over us? Oh no.
Authors' names were the library's filing system,
nothing more.
People were inside books on their own
like water inside a fire hydrant.
Whole cities and centuries in 2 inches of paper.
A pillar of water reaching the sky
and every child followed it
squealing to the promised land.
When I was about 15 everything was alive.
I could talk to trees and stones
and I believed what I read.
When I put my hands on a book
the cover was warm.
I could almost hear it breathing.

WATCHING THE NEWS

About equal time for Iraq and Michael Jackson.
Michael leads the troops
moonwalking into Baghdad
while pilots drop babies instead of bombs.
Undercover agents guard the madonna's blue dress
in case of Clinton stains.
We'll give all the perfumes of Arabia
to Laci Peterson's unborn child;
we'll find him by following yonder burning nightclub
to shepherds who've been in Iraq so long
the only names they know are their wives and their sheep,
and not always in that order.
We'll put duct tape over the child's mouth when he cries;
no child in the world will ever cry again,
we've got plenty of duct tape
and we're not afraid to use it.
The news is almost as silly as the commercials.
Dead soldiers wash their shrouds with this detergent.
This breakfast cereal can be eaten thru a gas mask.
This storage company will find a place
to put the war.
And if the dead aren't 100 percent satisfied
with this weight loss plan,
just return for a guaranteed refund.

FOR THE 50ᵀᴴ ANNIVERSARY OF GINSBERG'S HOWL

Ginsberg is a truck smuggling illegal aliens
over the borders of poetry.
Young men ready to do jobs Americans don't want,
climbing thru sewers of song, turning their tears into wine,
hanging hangovers on flagpoles and saluting.
No one's more alien than an alienated poet
bitch-slapped by morning light, every morning.
Ginsberg is a truck smuggling illegal aliens past walls of paper
guarded by gun towers and attack dogs,
leaping at the groins of de-construction workers,
who give lines impossibly long erections,
scattering words like their neon-bright seed all over the page.
Ginsberg is a truck made of flowers,
a float in the Gay Pride parade floating in mid-air
surrounded by buddhist sages also floating and chanting.
The truck is packed with naked lovers,
now floating in each other's arms.
Ginsberg is a truck smuggling illegal aliens
thru scorched rocks and tumbleweed,
but he's not a coyote whose nose knows the desert for a price.
Ginsberg is the Coyote God
and woe to all who take his name in vain.
They shall suffer from disgraceful fits of giggles
unto the 7ᵗʰ generation.
Ginsberg is a truck that knows no borders.
He's been up and down Jacob's ladder
and spouted with whales under the sea
and he never runs out of gas.
Ginsberg is a truck smuggling the future,
yes, Virginia, there is a future.
The door is open.
The key's in the ignition.
Get in.
Drive.

THE SON OF WAR

When they crucified the Son of War
they stripped off his uniform and nailed him
to the naked back of Mary Magdalene,
standing upright with slender outstretched arms.
Mary sings the same coaxing tune she'd sung the troops
when they march past her window,
her full breasts spilling from her red dress.
The Son of War knew it all too well.
When they crucified the Son of War
his hands were naked of weapons,
much worse than his naked body.
He could almost hear his sergeant
dressing him down in front of his squad
while he tries to stand at attention
with Mary Magdalene's noble and familiar rump
warmly squeezed against his own.
"Soldier, you think that machinegun your government paid for
is like your keychain or your lighter
and they'll be a Lost and Found
in the middle of the next battle?
Soldier, you're an insult to your country,
without your weapon you don't exist.
I'm staring right at you soldier
and nobody's there."
The Son of War tries to squirm with shame
but the nails hold him still.
When they crucified the Son of War
a rosevine grew from his spilled blood
wrapping round him and Mary;
thorns and scented petals press into every inch of them.
When the roses open there are faces inside.
The Son of War's dead buddies,

one rose stunk of beer farts and dirty jokes.
The girl back home in a pale pink rose
spits at Mary Magdalene. Mary laughs.
When they crucified the Son of War
the heavens opened for him
but all the saints sang Mary Magdalene's song
and saints shouldn't know such words,
much less sing them.
When they crucified the Son of War
he turned away from heaven
looking for a place where he belonged.
It had been so long he'd forgotten the words
but he was looking for a place of peace.

PLASTIC SKELETON

I've got a plastic full length skeleton
dangling from my ceiling at the foot of my bed.
The Boy Scout's motto: Be Prepared.
He's supposed to glow in the dark
but he doesn't.
I hung him with bright colored carnival beads,
some from his shoulders,
like Larry King's red suspenders,
most from his hips and dangling down his legs.
Orange, yellow, purple.
I wrapped a few strings of gold paper stars thru his ribs
and put a long black feather in his wristbones,
since I couldn't tie it to his fingers.
When the window's open to the wind
he turns slowly on his string
watching me from every angle,
judging.
Is the meat ready yet?
No, not yet.

16

FISHERS OF MEN

A reporter went to interview
a little fishing village right next to a road
both armies were fighting for.
The reporter had to walk thigh deep
into water wearing his good suit
'cause the fisherman was casting
and wouldn't come out.
"Well," the fisherman nodded
"at first we were angry.
All that noise was bound to scare off the fish
and we live off our fish.
Couldn't they kill each other somewhere else?
But then a funny thing.
A lot of blown-off limbs wound up in the water
and the fish ate them.
The fish got big, fat and careless,
didn't flick away from our shadows
when a floating hand was only dessert.
Not whole bodies, those were left
for bottom feeders and barnacles.
But the fish are huge now and our healer says
they're better than herbs for most childhood sicknesses
and a paste of the fishskin
will help a woman conceive sons.
Your armies here to bring freedom?"
he asked the reporter, "well, send more.
Freedom's good for the fishes."
He switched his attention back to his panting catch
almost too fat to struggle.

JERUSALEM WASHES HER HAIR

I saw Jerusalem washing her hair
in all the tears wept for her.
She stood under a roaring Niagara of grief
rubbing long fingers thru her dark wet prayers,
leaning her head back.
All faiths steamed over her shining skin.
Tears pounded down her bare shoulders.
Jerusalem took off a dress of broken promises
to wash her hair. All those betrayals
unfolding from all that beauty
which is also a betrayal.
We look at Jerusalem, want her,
we bring her funeral roses
and the weeping never stops.
Wailing voices kiss her stone lips
and the stones in her Wailing Wall.
Mothers rock dead children in a blanket of blood,
singing lullabies and little baby names
they've used for comfort;
if those names were on the death certificates
would there be as many death certificates?
Probably.
Suicide teenagers trying to marry Jerusalem, exploding,
their body parts thrown like bridal bouquets.
I've seen their pictures, they're all smiling,
surely youth can do anything.
Old scholars who turn their lives into nets of talmudic tales,
they usually keep their tears in wine bottles
but Jerusalem washes her hair
and they can't bear being old.
In ancient churches stained glass saints
weep glass tears shattering under Jerusalem's bare feet.
A farmer whose olive trees walked past the border,
the olives are ripe and ready for his hands

but there are sentries, he doesn't understand;
he gulps back a tear.
Even the guns weep and skeletons under the earth
who should've forgotten her.
Jerusalem washers her hair and rubs it
in a tangle of crumpled flags,
whatever comes to hand.
Then Jerusalem spreads it out on her hills to dry,
more lovely than her wildflowers.
Darker than any chance of peace.

19

STAR WARS

The new Star Wars movie just opened
and I squeaked onto section 8 housing
but I think the government would rather use my rent money
to buy light sabers for every soldier in Iraq.
There's no stars in the wars here, often no light.
Darth Vader sends out pink slips
when factories close.
Why can't we have a soundtrack?
Boys who see Star Wars come out wanting to save the world
but walk past appeals for AIDS
and a drunken veteran in a wheelchair
sparechanging. His pants legs hang empty.
I can't help him either but I can make him a star.
In a galaxy far, far too near
he was going to be married.
She had red hair, freckles, no particular gift for silence
and she couldn't keep her hands off him.
His phantom limbs itch with the weight of her body,
there's not enough drink in the world to make him forget.
Sure, he stole his kid brother's train set once
and left it in their backyard beech tree.
The kid worshiped him, really it was sorta boring.
There'd been a job waiting
but not for a man in a wheelchair.
Can we put his face on a coffee mug or a t-shirt?
Once upon a time in a galaxy far, far too near
look what happens.
Where are the stars of peace?

FOR MOE WHO DIED

I keep thinking it's an April fool's trick
and Moe'll come back growling contemptuously
over his cigar,
"You people'll believe anything,
whadda you mean, dead?"
I've still got a Moe's trade slip, Moe money
with his picture and the slogan
"in God and Moe we trust."
I'll feel funny about using it now.
I never minded George Washington being dead
but some people just aren't supposed to die.
I remember Moe's voice loudly unharmonizing
with whatever blues the ceiling was playing.
"She done him wrong" would drift upstairs
and splash over the book I was browsing,
hunched on a stool or pouring thru the rickety carts.
I remember the continual cheerful grumble
that came out of Moe like cigar smoke
and of course the cigars.
Freud said "sometimes a cigar is just a cigar"
but not now.
I want all cigars to have Moe's face on the gilt band.
I want Berkeley's no-smoking ordinance to go up in cigar smoke
at Moe's memorial, they can reinstate the silly thing
afterwards, if they have to.
I want to plant cigars on Moe's grave instead of flowers
and see what grows, something will.
I want exploding cigars.
I want to watch the endangered whales
blow waterspouts out of Moe's bald spot.
I want every book in all 4 floors of Moe's bookstore
to be about Moe because I don't know much about him
and never needed to before,

he'd obviously always be there.
I want Moe back.
I recognized Moe's photo in the shop window,
it's from the employees' bathroom
and it's one of a pair of photos in the same frame.
The other photo shows Moe with his back to the camera,
facing the john.
And I want that other photo to be in the shop window.
I want to see Moe pissing all over that April fool Death
that fools everyone.

BREAST CANCER SCARE

Kaiser left several messages on my answering machine.
It had been too many years since my last mammogram.
They told me how lucky I was
to be offered yearly mammograms
on their wonderful plan
and they bullied me into an appointment.
I finally went, mainly to stop the messages.
The woman who did the mammogram positively chirped
while her big steel machines beat up my breasts
in ways a man could get arrested for.
2 days later I got a call,
they'd found something.
Maybe a cyst, maybe not.
I should come right back to wonderful them
and they'd do an ultrasound.
They'd get me an appointment that afternoon.
That afternoon? This was Kaiser.
I must be dead.
The living wait at least 2 days.
I freaked. I called a friend
who told me what to expect
and tried to calm me down.
I got the ultrasound. It was Friday.
They couldn't show it to the radiologist till Monday,
she'd get in touch with my regular doctor,
I'd probably hear by Wednesday,
have a nice day.
I went home.
Since I was dead I got myself a huge slab
of bittersweet chocolate
but it tasted like cardboard.
The phone rang. It was the radiologist
who was going on vacation Monday

and thought she'd better call me first.
I should come back in 6 months as a formality
but my chart looked benign
and I should also ignore a scare letter I'd get.
When she hung up I started breathing
and the air tasted better than chocolate
until I took a second bite of chocolate.
I had my breasts back.
I pulled down the shades, stripped to the waist
and closed my eyes.
Everyone, from the red-haired boy
who wouldn't talk to me in grade school,
to Mick Jagger, to the young Brando playing Stanley
and to Bela Lugosi in his Dracula fangs
grabbed my breasts, bit them, sucked and played,
tweaked and kissed until I moaned.
They held me. I held me.
I'm old. My breasts sag.
But they're mine again. Mine.

PASSOVER IN JERUSALEM

Jerusalem watched a family celebrating Passover
in a house of good smells.
Death in the streets, death in the air,
music at the table.
"They still say 'next year in Jerusalem' she mused,
"but they are in Jerusalem, I am Jerusalem
and I also say next year.
What are we all waiting for?"
Then she shook her head as if afraid of an answer
and her marvelous dark prayers fell loose
shadowing her troubled face.
The eldest child paused in the middle of the 4 questions
he'd memorized that afternoon
and reached his unrealistically clean hands to Jerusalem's hair
while a very different question trembled on his lips.
"Why," he whispered, but didn't finish.
"There is blood on the doorpost as always
for the Angel of Death to pass over" Jerusalem continued
"but there is also blood on the street
and the last time I saw the Angel of Death
he'd gone blind.
Soft pearly cataracts covered the holes in his skull.
I asked him why but he only laughed."
"Too many people confuse me with Justice these days," he answered
"and isn't Justice blind?'
Jerusalem sighed. "I just stood there," she whispered
"in all my useless beauty."
The family poured the wine and boasted of the Lord's miracles
as proudly as they boast of good marks
their children got in school.
"Why?" asked Jerusalem, but didn't finish.

WAR

Two 9-year-olds loaded their toy guns
with summer cherries
and shot black red satin ripe at each other.
The stains were purple not red but they agreed
"close enough for government work".
They'd just heard the phrase
and tried it on everything.
When they got bored arguing whose turn it was
to play dead, they ate all the bullets,
seeing how far they could spit the pits
and sticking out purple tongues.
They'd raided the bathroom for pink fluffy towels
to make slings for imaginary wounds
but the towels kept coming untied.
Then the older boy decided the cherry stain
on his upper lip was a mustache
but the other boy couldn't have a mustache
'cause he was too young. (2 months younger).
The other boy started to cry
and their mother came out
and ruined everything.
They'd been having such a nice war.

FOR MY 60TH BIRTHDAY

60 years. I'm naked with folding days and nights,
years and decades slipping thru my arms
like shiny material for a dress I'll never make.
I pricked my thumb with Sleeping Beauty's needle
and sleep less and less.
The hedge of thorns grows under my skin.
But I'm not waiting for a licorice prince,
my bed's been rumpled by Rumpelstiltskin.
Goblins gobble my sagging nipples.
Waking up alone I see a pirate flag
disappearing from my belly button
and kisses crawl thru my hair like heavenly cockroaches.
My lovers don't live in time and treat me like a silly child:
"We brought you candy, open wide." I do. Yes.
60 years. I thought I'd know things
but things know me.
I thought I'd give the ocean good advice
and knit a jacket for the wind
and sing a lullaby to a black garden stone
that can't forgive the sprawling, scented roses.
I wanted wisdom.
I'd made a reservation at the Last Supper.
The Buddha lifted an empty bowl for me to drink
and the Passover plate left outside for Elijah
had enough for 2, I was on my way.
But my lovers dragged me behind some bushes
and did unspeakable things with Kentucky Fried Chicken,
crunching my thoughts like potato chips
and leaving me in a gasping heap.
I didn't know where I was but I hadn't tried to run away.
I wanted wisdom but what wanted me
laughs at wisdom, rudely, and waggles its tongue.
60 years. Each year I'm born again
and never get it quite right.
My lovers eat me like a birthday cake
and lick their lips.

GOD'S VIOLIN

Good and evil are only high and low
on one string of god's violin.
There are other strings being played
stretching from our guts to the end of the world.
Telephone wires vibrate with what we meant to say,
explanations lost in black curved space
like socks lost under the bed.
Our silences wail under god's fingers.
Our silences harmonize with
the implacable pastel rise of a department store
and its peacock tail of blind mannequin eyes
while the triumphal march of a snail
to the other end of its glossy leaf
plays counterpoint.

I dreamed god's violin.
The number of strings went on beyond
my eyes counting curve
and the length of the strings simply went on.
We miss so much.
Have you ever been driving alone at night
down a freeway fighting sleep
and chasing the white line?
Supposed you realized
no matter how long and fast you drove
you'd be stuck in one white mark on the white line
and never get past it.
Like that.

The Music of the Spheres.
The Fiddler on the Roof.
The Piper on the Hills.
The heart-tug behind tv commercials
before they start selling glop.

We don't hear god's violin because we're part of it
the way construction workers don't hear their own drills.
But sometimes, just for one or two notes
an echo sweeps us up like a tidal wave
scattering everything we clutch and fight for
out of our hands like spilled popcorn
and we stand in the ruins and laugh.
Afterwards we don't remember.
Or we pretend we don't remember,
putting everything wearily back the way it was
and going on
and that also goes into the music.

God's violin doesn't help anything,
the world's wounds are part of the music
and anyway, it's too big.
Like smashing a symphony hall complete with symphony
on top of a spoonful of cough medicine
for a sick child.

Maybe we're not supposed to listen.
Maybe it's not possible to really listen
and still be any use to our lives.
Like trying to touch a toolkit
with burnt, aching fingers.
But I've heard the roar of that fire in the strings
and reached for it
and couldn't reach high enough
and that was worse.
God's violin is for us,
what we are for
god only knows.

STEWED SOULS

34

PUNK GIRL IN THE COFFEEHOUSE

About 19, sitting in the coffeehouse,
a little plump, pink cotton candy hair.
She looks fresh like a warm frosted pastry
so deep in whipped cream conversation
with her friends you could walk by,
break off a few waving green-tipped fingers,
dunk them in your coffee and eat them
and she wouldn't even notice
till the next time she reached
for her death cigarettes.
She's just out of the grimy oven
of her black leather jacket
smelling cookie warm but still a little too moist.
If you touched her skin you'd leave a dent.
She talks in gasps of laughter,
passing her breath around
like gold-wrapped chocolates.
"More," she gurgles, "take more."
A bursting black negligee
shiny as the top of an eclair
and swinging gumdrop necklaces,
red, orange, and purple.
Her bare arms and soft throat
are white as melted marshmallows.
Every bite of her will stick to your fingers.
You'll have to lick her off them,
slowly.

REMEMBERING THE CAFE BABAR
POETRY READINGS

It was a little jazz bar in the Mission.
There was a picture of Babar the elephant
with his lady Celeste
on the big window we couldn't open,
and pretty soon
everyone was calling us the Babarian poets
with the accent wrong.
The hall was crammed with people trying to get in
so no one could get to the bathroom
even when there weren't lovers
using it for privacy.
No stage. No spotlight. No microphone.
We were nose to nose with the audience
and we were on our own.
Raw wooden boards for benches
that easily unbalanced, and if you stood up
you'd never see your seat again. Cheap beer
and when too many glasses smashed in anger
or homage: "Best fucking poem I've ever heard!" Crash—
Alvin the bartender got us huge paper cups.
We overthrew the government, love, time, death
and each other, all before the break
when we charged at the bar
or clustered outside for air
glancing up a little scornfully
at the dim night stars.
"I'm really shining tonight,
did you hear me shine?
You don't look so big."
We could leap tall buildings in a single bound
and buildings leapt after us, dancing.
The churches with lightbulb crosses.
The latenight burrito joints

with black velvet bullfighters and hotsauce.
Bart stations where gang graffiti's replaced
with billboards bought by bigger gangs
while an old man sits on a pail
and plays a quavering saw for quarters.
All these places danced with us and more.
We were so strong we had to destroy ourselves,
nothing else could touch us. So we did.
We were so American we got eaten
while Mom's hot apple pie congealed,
stood up at the diner.
We scared the socks off Auntie Death
who went after the poets.
Dead of O.D., dead of heart attacks,
dead of falling on a bar of soap
while climbing the sky.
But when there was a good poem
nobody breathed anyway.
On a good night we lived forever.

DEATH SINGING TO YOUNG MEN

Come lovers, leave your flesh-flower girls
weeping on mattress dents you made,
moaning through their sweaty curls.
I'll hold you closer as you fade,
black blood dancing on a blade
and you will stay where you are laid.

Come lovers to my singing worms.
Burn in my bed as a city burns
naked of clothes, naked of names.
In my arms there is no blame.
I'll hold you closer as you fade,
black blood dancing on a blade
and you will stay where you are laid.

Come lovers to my endless dance,
you won't leave me here alone?
Clutch your girl but feel my glance
then let me turn you into stone.
I'll hold you closer as you fade,
black blood dancing on a blade
and you will stay where you are laid.

BLUES FOR AMERICA

Sing blues for America, for big trucks
chasing the white lines all night
in every state on the mirror,
hauling heavy wooden boxes
nailed shut over our eyes.
America must not see. America, don't look
Sing boogie-woogie bug-eyed monster
uneasy to assemble blues for America,
will schoolchildren memorize the bill of wrongs?
Play spoons for nameless junkies cooking spoons
over a candle and America's greasy spoons
where nametagged peroxide waitresses call everyone "ducky".
Will government ghosts come to collect our names
while chattering waitresses collect our plates?
Sing blues for America.
Highstepping highways, fender kissing,
jelly-belly traffic jam blues for America,
fast cars, slow roads, leaning on horns.
A saxophone plays without pity
as pot roast and potatoes drift out of reach,
sing America drifting out of reach.
Sing rusty fire-escapes stretched
with laundry lines like fiddle strings,
walked on by mangy alley cats
and spangled circus acrobats.
Listen to laundry late at night,
boxer shorts and bathrobes sing blues for America leaving us,
America, don't go.
Drive-in horror movie background music
wails blues for America
with couples pretending terror in each other's arms,
knocking over half-empty popcorn boxes
and getting their knees tangled in the gear shift.
The 20 foot screen's full of blood and slime
but time stops when they kiss.
It's a small town, there are shotgun weddings,

but he's not to take his shotgun to war,
oh no, America, oh no.
Sing honky-tonk tacky blues for America.
Souvenir postcards of the Grand Canyon
with a Holiday Inn address on the back.
Give me some more of that old-time piano
and answer me this:
if we drop bombs just as deep all over the world
is the Grand Canyon still a wonder?
Will tourists still come with cameras?
Will we hear the center of the earth sing to the sky
or will we only sing blues for America?
Sing blues for a man standing in lines all day
and not getting work, coming home angry
and throwing a plate at the wall
because the food was overcooked,
next week he'll hit her
because he doesn't have work
and she's not looking at him but she might.
And he holds her all night
to hide from her eyes.
America, he thinks it's all his fault.
Sing blues for America, the land he loves,
the land we love.
America, come back.

POETRY

Poetry, he drives a creaky garbage truck
thru streets before dawn.
I knew it was Poetry cause his fingernails were dirty
from burrowing through mud at the full moon,
long ago.
I saw Poetry with a broken green glass wine bottle
lifted from under pizza boxes, tampons, flies and fishbones.
Poetry, he shut his eyes and saw the party: drunken songs,
a fight, a maybe girl and the stars spinning
like a tilt-a-whirl. Then he touched the jagged edge,
and one drop of Poetry blood fills the bottle;
yeah Poetry turns wine back into blood.
Will you drink?
Old photo albums wind up in his garbage truck
and Poetry looks thru cold chinese noodles
at faces when they were still in love
before he worked too late or screaming custody battles.
Poetry, he takes what you never want to see again.
Mattresses with their guts dangling out
like gunshot victims in old westerns
give up their ghosts to Poetry.
Mattresses know lots of ghosts.
Poetry, he don't work for the city.
He dumps your garbage onto a blank page.
You don't recognize it.
You call it beautiful.

CHILDREN PLAY JUMP-ROPE WITH JERUSALEM'S
HAIR DURING WARTIME

Jerusalem lies on her side,
leaning her prayer-laden head on one soft hand
and letting children play jump-rope with her long dark hair
while rockets screech overhead.
Jerusalem sees thru living children and dead children
to bombs falling like burning angels
on both sides of her screaming border
where there's no place to hide,
but Jerusalem only listens to jump-rope rhymes.
Children chant kisses up a tree
or how many guns burst into blossom
and point your toes
and if you stop you lose your turn.
None of the children look at Jerusalem
but her shadowed eyes rest on sharp elbows and bouncing knees
as if she played spin-the-bottle with them,
as if she could still play,
as if bottles weren't molotov cocktails out hunting bones.
Jerusalem does not ask dead children how they died.
Jump-ropes spin and children count toy soldiers.
Every toy soldier has a human shadow, killing and dying.
This is war and if you stop you lose your turn,
and if you stop you lose.
Jerusalem's shining hair twists into a noose to hang the sun
for the unforgivable sin of seeing her like this.
Children's jump-ropes count love letters
they're way too young for, even the dead children
so they put letters in cracks of the Wailing Wall
or wrapped around a stone to throw at a head,
but this is love and if you stop you lose your turn,
and if you stop you lose.
Jerusalem feels the tug on her heavy hair

and catches a shuddering breath,
all her beauty vibrates like a plucked fiddle string
in an empty house.
Jerusalem pulls her head away.
The jump-rope rhymes unravel and the children scatter,
the living and the dead
arguing who won.

PLAYING THE LOTTERY

I bought a lottery ticket
and before it didn't win
I was 2 people, me
and my fabulously rich twin.
She hired a limousine
and street people piled in,
shoving, hooting and hanging out the window
to give the finger.
We went to a fancy restaurant
that didn't want to let us in
but my rich twin slapped their faces
with a wad of hundreds
and ordered pink champagne for everyone
and roast duck flambé, caviar and just like the ad
all that cheese
which drunks smeared into each other's beards
and their girlfriends licked it off, giggling.
My rich twin, she bought out an entire Rolling Stones concert
for welfare mother's sons. Either sell the tickets
for 6 months of a better life,
the heat finally on, medicine, paid bills,
new clothes, schoolbooks
or one night of glory.
Never forgotten.
My rich twin, she bought a pair of senators
kept them on a leash and put them thru their paces
like poodles. They made laws like doodoo
when she took them walking in the morning.
The laws changed things.
Soon one-room residential hotels grew up
in cheap creaking dignity all over the country.
Old people sat in the lounge like bent umbrellas
telling their lives like Buddhist monks tell beads.
Sometimes I listened.
I bought a lottery ticket. No, it didn't win
but oh, the memories.

CRONE

When I was about 9 I saw a silver ring
in a jeweler's window.
And I wanted it, but not to wear.
It had a small turreted silver castle on the band
and the top of the highest tower
was a dark red garnet.
I knew that garnet was the curved roof of a room
where I'd live when I was old, very old,
as old as I am now.

Everyone in the castle would be a little afraid of me
and leave my meals in front of my door
on tiptoe
and tell strangers I'd died long ago.
They'd know I watched them
when I remembered about people
which I didn't always.
What would people matter to an old woman, very old,
as old as I am now?

I'd stand at my window and raise storms,
I loved to hear the lightning laugh.
Or I'd snake my tongue out for a drop of rain
that never reached the earth
and let the fine wines sour outside my door.
I'd do magic like knitting or a jigsaw puzzle
just to keep my hand in
and the edge behind my eyes.
I'd turn the cheese in rattraps to crown jewels
just to learn new swear words from the rats.
When I was about 9 I stared at that silver ring
and saw myself an old woman, very old,
as old as I am now.

At one time I bought an identical ring,
never wore it
and watched the garnet get dusty.
It got lost when I moved.
I did learn new swear words from rats
but people still matter.
I'd like to tell that 9 year old
she's the only one
who's ever lived in that tower room.
All those cobwebbed years in the 2 minutes
she smudged her nose against the jeweler's window.

BASEBALL

Not the school games.
There was a vacant lot at the end of the second block
where the bases were rocks,
second base in particular tore jeans and bloodied knees.
And there was a hedge of dead mustard taller than we were
that the girls watched behind.
Not the game and certainly not the boys
but we weren't wanted so of course we came.
Wild mustard twigs caught in our hair
while we caught our breath.
Any child can smell a secret.
At school there was clean school equipment
but the ball in the vacant lot
used to belong to a boy's brother
who died in the war.
The boy snuck in and stole it
while his mother donated everything else to Goodwill.
This was a stolen, badwill ball
that Death spat on for luck.
When that ball flew high
caverns of sky collapsed behind it
and it looked like the sun was falling.
Most of the girls didn't even know the rules.
There wasn't an umpire.
Most of the boys could've been making up the rules
as they went along.
It didn't matter.
In his grave the dead boy chanted:
"batter, batter, batter up".

THE STORY OF CHERRIES

I roll summer cherries in my palm,
ripeblack and much too rich
to grow on trees.
I close my eyes
and see a pirate ship after a raid,
the deck overflowing with spilled gold coins
and the king's favorite bellydancer
naked in the center
with only a ruby in her navel.
She has a suffocation of black hair
and a stilled, dangerous face like a dagger
waiting for the killing hand.
The pirates' eyes scuttle over her swaying breasts
like wasps.
The captain waves to a little man with bad teeth
hunched over a squeaky fiddle
and commands her to dance for them,
to dance first.

The ruby flashes, she leans backwards,
her slow hips clang together and apart
like a churchbell tolling for the dead.
Her raised leg points
at a gull hovering overhead;
this is the first time she's been outside
since the king's soldiers stole her.
As the dance ends she shakes her belly
and the ruby falls out,
becomes a cherry
followed by many cherries
rolling over the slippery deck.

The pirates grab them in rope-roughened handfuls,
scuffling with each other.
The cherries' skin is softer than the girl's.
The cherries' flesh is cool.
The dancer crouches, leaps, turns into a gull
and swoops off towards the sun.
The pirates yell after her
and their boots trample the cherries.
Red-purple stains everywhere
as from a bloody battle.
That's the story of cherries,
summer cherries in my palm,
not quite too beautiful to eat.

JERUSALEM WALKED THRU WAR

Jerusalem walked thru war
whistling for a pack of dogs
barking like guns,
whistling for a pack of guns
barking like dogs
to relieve themselves by firehydrants
and spilled brains.
"M16, you pretty little thing,
wag your tail
and do your business."

Jerusalem walked thru war
among crumpled bodies
and stole their bloody clothes.
"My lovers should always be naked," she explained.
"I bury them in a soft shroud of kisses
but my lips cannot forgive
that none of them kiss me back.
Am I not beautiful?"

Jerusalem walked thru war,
thru burning ruins:
from a little Arab market
with scorched oranges rolling in the dust,
to the Church of the Nativity
where saints' stained glass faces
cough from the smoke,
to the child's bloody stroller at the Passover massacre.

Jerusalem sings to make the flames dance.
She rubs the back of her hand against charred wood
and draws sooty black hearts on any wall still standing.
Jerusalem walked barefoot on ashes
like sand on the beach, wriggling her toes.
Jerusalem walked thru war.
War walked thru Jerusalem.

THE DEVIL

Yes, I've met the devil, most people have,
he gets around.
Not at the crossroads at midnight
and I didn't summon him with rituals.
I've got nothing to sell,
I can't call my soul my own
since I started writing.
But I've got a big dark leather chair
in the corner of my room
and last night there was a darker shadow in it.
He laced gloved fingers together
and looked over them at me as if I were a fireplace
for his dancing memories.
"I fell from loving God too much, not from pride,"
he whispered, like a schoolboy at his first confession.
"I can't share God, I never could.
I don't want his throne; I want him.
When heaven and earth and all of you are destroyed
he'll have no one left to love but me.
I can wait."
He was about to disappear then changed his mind.
"I can't expect you to understand," he shrugged.
"I'm called the Father of Lies and I lie to you
but never to myself.
No angel can, however fallen.
While you,
you lie to yourselves all the time.
What can you know about love?"

THE JACK MICHELINE MEMORIAL

There were about 500 people
packed into the Jack Micheline memorial
and it was hot, sweaty, stuffy.
I went outside to get some air
and bumped into Jack Micheline
who was complaining.
All those people he'd known so long,
whenever there was a really big Beat bash
with food, booze, famous people and the press
he got passed over.
He had to hear about this one
from a drunk in a bar down the street
and *he'd* known Kerouac,
he bet he'd known whoever died
better than everyone wearing out the mike.
"Well yeah," I said
and wondered how to go on.
"Besides," he continued, "if he'd known
he coulda brought books to sell,
it was a really big crowd
and he was broker than usual.
Or trade a painting for a place to crash.
He wasn't feeling the cold
for some reason
but after all it was San Francisco."
"Yeah," I said again.
Death hadn't changed him
and there was no way I could tell him.
I waited for him to charge the doorway
like an aging elephant,
swaying his righteous belly

and shouting poems in all directions.
But he didn't.
He just shrugged and grinned
at how unfair it all was
and headed down a dark alley.
Maybe back to the drunk
who'd told him about the memorial
and hadn't known who it was for.

JERUSALEM DURING A SUICIDE BOMBING

Jerusalem strolled thru an outdoor market
during a suicide bombing.
It rained fingers and oranges
and blood bright as summer cherries.
Strawberry ice cream cones blew straight up
and knocked birds off their course,
then fell back on a little boy's scabbed knee,
the rest of him was gone.
The wind of the blast
blew thru Jerusalem's prayers,
her hair roared back like a lion,
like 2 lions mating in mid-air.
Jerusalem's eyes half-closed,
her lips parted, gasping a little,
lost in the moment like any woman in a bed.
Ritual men with bags go thru the scene
collecting body parts
to be buried together like jigsaw puzzles
but Jerusalem is a puzzle whose pieces change shape
when the wind blows.
She smiles and yawns,
her hills breathing like breasts.
Jerusalem remembers when it rained frogs
and men fought
in chariots with swords
and died calling her name.
Feathers knocked off birds that don't care
wind up pressed between pages
of the Books of the Law.
Jerusalem's naked feet leave the scene of love,
nothing changes.

CANNIBAL MUSIC

Cannibals wearing necklaces of knucklebones,
facepaint, and nothing else
only kill as many people as they can eat.
They dance around the fire while tattooed women
their long hair strung with large amber beads
season the screaming meat with pineapples, mangoes,
papayas, onions, wild mushrooms and hot peppers.
After a battle they'll keep prisoners for future meals
but not too many—
bound men without guns are just an invitation to wolves
and wolves take cannibals' children.
They love their children and sharpen their teeth into points
and give them a pile of vertebra for building blocks.
Cannibals eat every day, that's a lot of people.
The cooking pot is always hungry.
But not as many as civilized war.
No bomb victims, wasted meat covered with flies.
No minefields, small pieces blown in all directions,
not enough left for hors d'oeuvres.
No missiles aimed at a map, can't eat a map.
And cannibals don't torture anyone for information;
they fatten captives up into food for thought.
Cannibals love their food and don't hate anyone.
Cannibals sing at the smell of dinner cooking,
drumming and licking their lips.
Listen to their happy music.

PICKLED TONGUES

BILLY THE KID

Billy the Kid wasn't kidding around.
He shrugged himself thru history like a human cactus,
all that paper tore at his touch.
A book of thorns, grinning when he emptied his guns.
I had a history book in eighth grade
that was so boring it would've put sheep to sleep.
I'd come home and I'd do history homework
till I couldn't bear it anymore.
Then I'd put the book facedown
so numbing facts couldn't get out
and I'd go play with Billy and watch him kill people.
Billy shot people when he was drunk
or when they looked at him funny
but most of the time there wasn't a reason till afterwards
and it wasn't a good idea to ask.
Billy spun both smoking guns before putting them back
in their holsters and laughed.
He had a missing front tooth and freckles.
Billy ran his fingers thru his hair when he was hungry.
But I had to be back in time for dinner and history.
Memorize dates of battles and write a boring book report
pretending something happened in a war,
I can't remember which war.
I got older. I joined anti-war protests, marches,
speeches against senseless killing.
One night I dreamed of Billy the Kid.
He wasn't any older.
"Armies?" he scoffed, "these men take orders,
do you think I'd let anyone give me orders?
They're as bad as that posse getting up after me.
These poor fools kill people they're sent to kill;
a real man kills people he chooses for his own reasons."
"But Billy," I stammered, "you never had any reasons."

He looked at me as if I were crazy.
"I killed them because I wanted to, that's my reason.
Soldiers just want to go home
but they're stuck killing thousands more than I ever did
till someone else decides they can stop.
That's history.
All the books about it are the same.
If I was alive I might even join your protest,"
he winked at me.
"Killing should never be wasted
on people who can't appreciate it.
Send all the soldiers home
to take orders at work and sell things
and be polite to customers.
There's not many like me.
The wind is my country.
I'm pure as a rattlesnake.
You can come play with me anytime."

THE VICTORIANS

Victorians covered the legs of all furniture,
otherwise it was indecent.
They might walk into a room
and interrupt a pile of chairs
sweating and grunting at all angles
topsy-turvy with the musky smell of varnish.
And if there was a fate worse than death
there'd be a litter of illegitimate whimpering footstools,
probably purple with gold silk trim,
shamefully bright.
Then the victorians went to church
and the preacher was so outraged by sin
the victorians felt they'd spent their Sunday
rolling with the damned on their bed of fire.
The damned were naked, young and beautiful
but the victorians were wearing their Sunday best,
high lace collars, long dark clothes
and sleeves tight at the wrist like handcuffs,
just in case.
The devils had modeled for gargoyles on the church roof
so hell was homey and familiar,.
As children they'd had nicknames for the gargoyles.
The ceiling of hell was open to heavenly hosts peering in,
wings and music watching the damned writhe so sweetly
in the arms of victorians wearing their Sunday best.
To look at God they had to look past Lucifer
with his tail tickling between their legs
which was not their fault.
It was easier to close their eyes.
Afterwards a potluck brunch and gossip.
Forbidden apples made into apple pie.
And women felt even the blind eyes of potatoes
in the potato salad
staring thru their clothes. Women blushed.
Men put on their black leather riding gloves, smiled
and left no fingerprints.

PASSOVER

When the Angel of Death passed over
all the Hebrew families covered their eyes,
clutched their children and warned them not to look
but one little boy peeked.
It was almost too late.
Only a big shadow already gone
except for one impossibly long shiny black feather
fallen right outside his window.
He grabbed it before his mother could yell
"don't touch that, you don't know where it's been"
the way she always did.

The family was busy packing and they packed him
in a cart under some blankets.
At first he just wanted to breathe
and then he jumped off the end of the cart
and he left the whole procession leaving Egypt.
The only thing he took with him
was his father's bottle of ink
because it was black as the feather
clutched in his dirty fingers.

He spent the next 40 years in his own wilderness
writing stories the living left behind
tangled in Death's wings, in that one feather.
Sometimes he wrote on rocky cave walls
for archaeologists to get wrong.
Sometimes on sand till the wind blew.
It didn't matter.
He felt a great crowd with him always,
they weren't real
but they could shine a lizard as still
as headlights shine a deer.
He ate and wrote. He was a child.
Sometimes he'd stare at a cactus flower
and wonder about beauty.

It seemed to be important.
He'd been taught his prayers so he prayed,
still holding the feather.

After 40 years he stumbled into the promised land,
the wind blew his feather away
and he was still a child.
His family had mourned him long ago,
as one of many children eaten by desert animals.
He didn't go back to them.
There was an old woman in town
troubled in mind who needed care.
They looked at each other once,
her young eyes and toothless gums,
his schoolboy face.
They nodded and asked no questions.
He moved in.
Evenings, there was singing.

BABY ON THE BUS

The baby was crying so loud
his voice was bigger than the bus.
His mother tried to give him his bottle
but when he figured out he couldn't swallow
and yell at the same time
he threw the bottle indignantly
all the way to the driver's seat,
she was trying to steal his screams!
Another passenger brought the bottle back,
smiled, tried to make it all normal.
The mother was embarrassed, found a smile
that didn't fit, obviously wished
everyone who was pretending not to notice
would drop dead or go away.
She checked his diapers,
they didn't need changing, she wasn't surprised.
He wasn't screaming for her to do something,
he'd forgotten she existed.
He clenched his face, hit his stroller,
his small body screamed big enough for the world.
The world needs changing,
diapers full of dirty wars.
I had to get off the bus
but I can still hear that baby.
He's going to scream till we fix the world.

AN EXTRA THANKSGIVING WITH A FRIEND

His old friend back east finally died
thanksgiving morning.
Four of my friends died that year.
Neither of us felt particularly thankful.
He bought an 18 pound Safeway turkey before his friend died
but his oven died
so he asked if he could roast it at my place
the day after thanksgiving.
When his friend died he phoned me, gulping sobs,
and I asked if we should cancel or freeze the turkey
and do it later.
He said "hell, no."
This was war.
He made a complete gourmet thanksgiving dinner at his place
while the turkey roasted in my oven
and brought it over as a sort of a laughing revenge.
Cranberry sauce made with sourcream
and a piece of horseradish is a weapon against god.
God can't have any candied yams,
they're for me and him and our dead friends.
2 kinds of stuffing, one with cornbread and chestnuts;
god can go eat graves.
Homemade gravy is thicker than blood.
He was practically dancing in the kitchen.
He'd brought over his grandmother's silver,
she was a great lady also dead and dining with us.
And then the turkey was glisteningly ready
and my friend had forgotten the big carving knife.
It was cold, dark and somehow not safe to leave,
he might start crying again.
All he had was a boyscout knife smaller than his thumb.
I watched his face rumpling and remembered
I'd got a black double-edged SS dagger years ago
at the flea market and had it leaning against my window

next to stained glass and deer horns ever since.
So we carved a thanksgiving turkey with an SS dagger,
had 2 helpings of everything and watched dumb tv
till I went into the kitchen for some reason
and started yelling. The gas was still on,
my friend has no sense of smell,
we could've joined our dead right then.
We opened windows. My friend explained about old stoves.
I wasn't listening.
God had come to our thanksgiving,
the only thanksgiving in the entire country
where he wasn't invited.
Where he wasn't welcome.
I took another spoonful of mango sherbet
biting it with all my teeth.
"I can still taste it," I whispered under my breath,
"it tastes so good."

THE HOMELESS ARE OUR DIRTY UNDERWEAR

We've got to get the tired men
pushing broken shopping carts,
the waddling bag ladies
with plastic flowered raincoats,
and the skinny young kids sparechanging dogfood
for their dog and all her nuzzling puppies
off the street.
Off the street before the bombs fall.
I can't explain the connection
but I remember:
"Suppose you were run over by a truck
and when they undressed you in the morgue
and you were wearing that dirty underwear
in front of everyone
wouldn't you just die of shame?"
So when the bombs fall
everyone must be wearing clean underwear,
good clothes, looking well fed
and happily married in houses with gardens
and swings for the children
even when it isn't true,
hell, especially when it isn't true.
It's a matter of patriotism.
We have to suffer to look good enough for death,
like dressing for a job.
The homeless weren't American enough to live
and they're certainly not American enough to die.
They're such an embarrassment.
Suppose the world ends
and there's still broken shopping carts
in ruined cities?
Suppose the broken shopping carts never go away?

"OBVIOUSLY, WE SHOULD BUILD ANOTHER JERUSALEM NEXT DOOR, SO THEY'D STOP FIGHTING"
—a tv anchor

Jerusalem is the symbol
of why no one is ever satisfied.
She cannot be cloned
or turned into a theme park.
Canned cheerful music at the Wailing Wall,
giant mouse ears on the Dome of the Rock,
Dolly the sheep as the Lamb of God?
No.
There's no door next door.
How could you map her trembling
and give the maps to a scientist?
Jerusalem is not even like herself,
the wind blows in all directions
inside her very stones.
The dazzle of prayers tangle her perfumed hair,
"bless us and kill them"
"kill them and bless us".
Like a child's jump rope rhyme.
Jerusalem's beauty is a stain deeper than blood,
those who look at her cannot be at peace,
not with their neighbors
and never with themselves.
Jerusalem weeps during wars,
banging her fists against stars
till her knuckles bruise,
long sobs wrenching her body
like an angry lover
but she can't tell soldiers apart,
nobody has names, just screams.
I have been told the light in Jerusalem
is higher than anywhere else in the world.
Steven Spielberg can do any imaginable special effect
but Jerusalem is an unimaginable special cause.

There are so many people happy to die
and kill for her shadow,
and so many afraid to live in her shadow,
to juggle oranges for children
between the jaws of history,
to cook, hang out laundry and gossip
with her eyes looking thru us at god,
with god's eyes looking thru us at her.

FOR MY DEAD MOTHER

There is a dark forest in my room at night
just before sleep drinks my eyes.
My dead mother sits on the twisted branch of a spreading tree
brushing moonlight out of her long white hair
with the silver-backed brush she had when she was alive.
She doesn't need a mirror anymore.
She sings to a slinking wolf with his tongue half out
as if he could bite the music and how would it taste?
She sings to birds eating the trail of breadcrumbs
Hansel and Gretel left behind,
there's no way out of this forest.
She sang these songs to me when I was a child,
she does not sing to me now.
I can hear every leaf fall in the forest
and a pot boiling in the witch's hut
and a frog on a lilypad being oh so pleased with himself.
I watch my dead mother's lips move.
I cannot hear her sing.
She's not wearing her wedding ring
but on the lake swim 2 golden swans with long necks enlaced.
They were on the corners of my parents' 4-posted bed
when I was a child, before the hot anger and cold silences.
My dead mother sings white flowers open all over the tree,
a little wind nuzzles at her white blouse like a baby
and some of the flowers fall thru my dead mother's white hair.
Her dangerous dark eyes unmask every raccoon
and find out what it's been up to.
Her heavy raised eyebrows, soft as fur, outfox the foxes.
She never saw this bedroom
she's not seeing it now.
I can't see her anymore.

BOGEYMAN SAYS WE DO FEAR ALL WRONG

Bogeyman, he went for a walk in the world,
worms in his hair, hands in his pockets
where cold slime coats his claws soft as a glove.
His shadow's made of ravens, it keeps changing shape,
beaks open for blood.
Bogeyman, he went for a walk in the world
and he didn't like what he saw.
"Children's fear is good enough to eat
so I do," he smiled with way too many teeth.
"And I eat the children, from first choked scream
to last toe-wiggle.

But now everyone's scared
and they're doing it all wrong.
The alarm clock ticking them to work
is a terrorist bomb, it's just a matter of time
and time don't matter anymore.
If they act like they're already dead
they won't notice the difference so much.
Everyone's scared but there's no juice to their fear;
it tastes like hospital food
or those pumped up, half plastic tomatoes.
It's not even called fear,
it's 'being cautiously alert at all times'."

Bogeyman, he pulled a curved bone from his vest pocket,
lit it like a cigarette and started to smoke.
"Another rib of Adam," he explained. "Yes, I was there.
I ate no fruit but fear and found it good.
Fear makes hearts beat bright as love.
Couples cling in horror movies.
If this is your last breath
use it to swallow sun, moon, God and your first bicycle
while I swallow you."

Bogeyman, he blew out smoke blue as forget-me-nots.
"I went for a walk in the world," he continued
"you've been stealing my shiny, high and mighty fear
and cutting it with boring politics
then selling it like any street drug.
I've been playing with my children too long,
my dear little dead.
I know where you live."

LONELY

Ugly old Lonely's big calloused hands
go all over a shivering girl.
She can marry, take lovers, be a movie star
but her skin still aches with Lonely's darkening bruises.
Where he held her too hard.
Where he won't let go.
Lonely breathes heavy down a girl's throat:
phones that don't ring.
Clocks that tick all night.
Even when she's laughing and drinking champagne
Lonely's cold kiss coils under her tongue.
Lonely never sleeps. Neither does she.
Lonely's so old, he's made so many girls cry,
he knows too much.
He knows how to touch a girl
till her hands go blind;
Lonely's all her arms can find.

TELEGRAPH AVENUE AFTER THE CHAGALL SHOW

Chagall, how would you paint our streets?
3 punk boys not old enough to drink
sparechanging for beer for their mascot
Hank the rooster, who drank from the can
and always drank first.
Even sorority blondes stopped to stroke Hank's feathers
while the boys sat ankle-eye level
not quite brave enough to whistle
until the day Hank betrayed them all
and laid an egg.
Next day, they were gone.
Chagall, paint that egg like the sun
in your ferris wheel whirling blue sky
with the 3 boys hatching out, leather clad,
yolk splattering their hair,
climbing down arm over arm to your happy goats
with a village streaming between their legs.

The city took our bus benches away
because they were slept on at night.
Chagall, will you help white haired old ladies
with bags of groceries and kittylitter
whose ankles hurt from arthritis?
Paint wings for them, red, yellow, green,
bright as traffic lights
to hover above the sidewalk
and peer down the street over trucks
to see if their bus is coming yet.

Chagall, after a football game's won
paint red-faced drinkers clanking thick glasses
while pepperoni pizzas spin around their heads like haloes.
One of your watersellers
with a heavy stick across his shoulders

brings full pails of beer to their table
and a purple horse leaps out the window, snorting.

Your musicians can play on our streets.
King David's crown is made of shiny quarters,
crazy-glued together.
Even the black lace vampire goth girls
with skeleton earrings stop at his much-fingered harp
and slowly blush thru their death-white make-up.
King David's smile and harp
can turn any woman
into a woman
and it will get him in trouble here too.

Chagall, paint drunken roofs for our drunks,
paint roads curving into the sky with angels leaning over
to tickle red-veined noses till they sneeze.
If they get away from the cops
some drunks pass out in your pictures
and never know the difference.
Chagall, paint us home,
till even the textbooks under a student's arm
are full of magical young women
whose kisses leap into his mouth
and drag him bewildered into your bursting flowers
the moment he opens a page.

LOVERS IN A LITTLE ROOM

When they're all over each other
like the happiest train wreck
in the world,
the stone faces on Mount Rushmore
fill with hot air
and float like striped carnival balloons,
strings dangling down to jumping children.

When their mattress is stuffed with broken clocks
and they tell time only
by wriggling their toes,
the Statue of Liberty puts down her torch
and drapery
and goes skinny-dipping in the harbor,
coaxing incoming ships to tickle her nipples.

When they skinslide thru sweaty sheets,
tangled hair full of dancing frogs,
the opening Stock Exchange counts the returns
on Valentine's long-stemmed red roses
all over the world,
other investments forgotten.

When their flesh is soft and clingy
as enough magic mudpies
to feed all famine victims,
textbooks in history classes
turn to sticky taffy
and students read with eager tongues.

When their bodies clench like a baby's fist
wobbled at the morning sun

everything is possible.
Statues of famous generals
get off their pedestals
and help bag ladies feed the pigeons.
Armies are reassigned to wait outside Safeways
and help tired housewives carry packages home
and up 3 flights of stairs.
People open their eyes
as if we'd all been asleep for thousands of years
and never seen each other.
And we all look while a spring wind
sings thru our hair,
all except the lovers in their little room.
They've finally fallen asleep.

OLD MAN CROSSING THE STREET

Old man
drags his feet after a cane
slowly.
Light changes
half way across the street.
Cars screech to a halt,
lean on their horns,
yell out their windows,
give him the finger.
If anything
he slows down.
He's old.
He can barely
haul himself up the curb.
His grandchildren don't write.
But shiny new cars wait trapped
as his cane takes its time.
They hate him.
It makes him young.

FOR DAVID LERNER, DEATH OF A POET

300 pounds, laughing like the Loch Ness Monster,
about 6 foot 5 with 4 more inches
of a New York jewish afro and wide matching beard,
glasses scotch-taped together,
usually wearing green sweatpants
that made you look even larger and more rumpled.
You filled an elevator at Tom's art show
while horrified Warhol elegants clung to the corners,
their mirror shades ready to break
at the sight of your orange bowling shirt.
You were singing under your breath
"dum de deedle de dum".
You were so big
you couldn't quite fit in this world;
you had to make it bigger.
You shoved elbows thru history
looking for a place to sit
and rest your bad back.
You walked on your poems like Jesus walked on water.
You were almost religiously convinced
you could inconspicuously boost cigarettes
at the supermarket check out line. Oh well.
You'd occasionally proclaim someone god,
give them a 10 foot tall face filling your eyes
until you went for hamburgers
and forgot all about them.
The rest of us didn't exist
no matter how we squawked and yelped
until it was our turn:
"why didn't you tell me you were god?"
Totally exasperated as if we'd cheated you.
There was a bigger litter of lost gods behind you
than lost lighters,
and you always lost lighters.
You took advantage of your friends

and boasted about them.
When you got somehow rich you'd buy a big house
and we'd all live together
and have happy fights
and write poems hotter than the sun.
You didn't tie your shoelaces
and you thought people should prove they were worthy
to read your books.
You weren't patient enough for ordinary ambition,
you just wanted the sky to open
because you were a genius,
and the really irritating thing is
you *were* a genius.
You became a force of nature
by breaking as many natural laws
as legal ones,
sometimes you were chased by supernatural policemen
and demons.
Once you walked barefoot over the Bay Bridge
with 2 bags of laundry.
You rang my doorbell and said politely
you knew I worked for the Devil
but that was just my job
and would I look after your stuff
till things calmed down?
I gulped and said sure.
You were good with nuthouse phones,
you used them to fill phoney prescriptions
from imaginary doctors.
You made friends with other patients
like lost playmates from a childhood
none of you ever had.
You'd pulled your back moving furniture

which was a righteous reason to be strung out
but also you found junk lovely
and full of god.
Your lover finally left,
afraid you'd pawn her teddybear collection.
You were her biggest teddybear,
she wanted your children so bad
ghost children are playing marbles with your ghost right now,
you're probably all cheating.
You had a long rumbling laugh
with ships sailing across it;
they didn't always get to the other side.
You named your cat after a gangster,
wanted your very own army tank
to deal with traffic jams
and you even got a scrawled death threat
shoved under your door
several months after you'd died.
Talk about immortality.
And you'd stand swaying in that packed back room
while we squeezed forward,
we couldn't breathe from waiting
and you knew it.
So you'd light a cigarette, slowly,
before your first poem.

VALENTINE

I bought a rose, a red, red rose,
put it in a bottle and threw it out to sea.
Whoever finds it, there is no map,
no buried treasure, no secret decoder ring,
no invisible ink.
What's written on a rose, scented, long-stemmed
is easy to read.
If you look past the rose and see our battleships
ready to bomb the hanging gardens of Babylon
the rose is still there, cupped in your palm.
If the bottle breaks on the craggy rocks of Ireland
where the singing dead have no mercy
the rose has no mercy.
Love has no mercy.
If the rose washes up, living, in the Dead Sea
touch it with living hands.
Never take it to a grave.
Follow the curl of the partly open petals
with one finger. Gently.
The rose changes nothing.
Expect nothing.
It's for you.

Julia Vinograd is a Berkeley street poet. She has published 52 books of poetry, and won the American Book Award of The Before Columbus Foundation. She has three poetry CD collections: *Bubbles and Bones*, *Eye of the Hand*, and *The Book of Jerusalem*. She received a B.A. from the University of California at Berkeley and an M.F.A. from the University of Iowa. She received the 2004 Poetry Lifetime Achievement Award from the City of Berkeley. She was one of the four editors of the anthology *New American Underground Poetry Vol. 1: The Babarians of San Francisco— Poets from Hell*.

Selected titles available from Zeitgeist Press

The Bruised Angels' Almanac by **Susan Birkeland** $5.95
The Revolution of 1964 by **Jennifer Blowdryer & Lenore Waters** $5.95
Where's My Wife by **Jennifer Blowdryer** $5.95
Trek To The Top Of The World by **Andy Clausen** $5.95
The Cities of Madame Curie by **Laura Conway** $9.95
My Body Is A War Toy by **Joie Cook** $5.95
Some Angels Wear Black by **Eli Coppola** $13.95
Flying at Café Babar (CD) by **Eli Coppola** $10.00
As Needed For Rage by **David Gollub** $5.95
how sweet it is by **q. r. hand, jr.** $5.95
The Satin Arcane by **Jack Hirschman** $5.95
Ghosts Among the Neon by **Bruce Isaacson** $11.95
The Last Five Miles to Grace, by **David Lerner** $12.95
Pirate Lerner CD by **David Lerner** $10.00
The New American Underground Poetry: The Babarians of San Francisco–
Poets From Hell, ed. **Julia Vinograd, David Lerner, and Alan Allen** $23.00
Going For The Low Blow by **Vampyre Mike Kassel** $5.95
The Queen of Shade by **Sparrow 13** $5.95
Outlaw Of The Lowest Planet by **Jack Micheline** $8.95
Imaginary Conversation With Jack Kerouac by **Jack Micheline** $8.95
The Hummingbird Graveyard by **Maura O'Connor** $5.95
Poesy 30ᵗʰ Edition, Cafe Babar Issue, **Poesy Magazine** $2.00
Westering Angels by **Eliot Schain** $15.00
The Underwater Hospital by **Jan Steckel, M.D.** $5.00
When There's No More Room In Heck, The Darned
Will Walk The Earth by **Chris Trian** $5.95
Berkeley Street Cannibals by **Julia Vinograd** $8.95
Beside Myself by **Julia Vinograd** $8.95
The Cutting Edge by **Julia Vinograd** $8.95
Face to Face by **Julia Vinograd** $8.95
Skull & Crosswords by **Julia Vinograd** $8.95
Dogs In Lingerie by **Danielle Willis** $11.95
Tenderloin Rose by **Kathleen Wood** $5.95

Zeitgeist Press
1630 University Avenue #34
Berkeley, CA 94703 U.S.A.
Please add $1 per book for handling and postage or
order at: www.zeitgeist-press.com